D1456019

WHAT HAPPY COUPLES DO

Belly Button Fuzz & Bare-Chested Hugs

WHAT HAPPY COUPLES DO

The Loving Little Rituals of Romance

Carol J. Bruess, Ph.D. & Anna D.H. Kudak, M.A.

Published by Fairview Press, 2450 Riverside Avenue, Minneapolis, Minnesota 55454. Fairview Press is a division of Fairview Health Services, a community-focused health system, affiliated with the University of Minnesota. For a free current catalog of Fairview Press titles, please call toll-free 1-800-544-8207. Or visit our Web site at www.fairviewpress.org.

Library of Congress Cataloging-in-Publication Data
Bruess, Carol J., 1968-
  What happy couples do : belly button fuzz & bare-chested hugs : the loving little rituals of romance / by Carol J. Bruess & Anna D.H. Kudak.
    p. cm.
  Includes bibliographical references.
  ISBN-13: 978-1-57749-172-9 (pbk. : alk. paper)
  ISBN-10: 1-57749-172-6 (alk. paper)
  1. Marriage. 2. Married people. 3. Man-woman relationships. I. Kudak, Anna D.H., 1982-
II. Title.

  HQ734.B9132 2008
  306.81—dc22

                          2007031718

Printed in China
First Printing: January 2008
12 11 10 09 08   5 4 3 2 1

Cover design: Tanya L. Watkins
Interior design: Natalie Nowytski, Renaissance Jane

For Brian and Brent, with whom we enjoy the best in life
(and a whole lot of loving little rituals).

— Carol & Anna

Share Your Stories

If you are inspired by the stories in this book and have your own
stories and rituals that will inspire others, please tell us about them!
Visit www.whathappycouplesdo.com and click on *Share Your Stories.*
We would love to hear what you are DOing in your marriage so that
we might share it with others. Or you can e-mail us:
Carol Bruess: carol@whathappycouplesdo.com
Anna Kudak: anna@whathappycouplesdo.com

How *beautiful* THIS THING CALLED MARRIAGE CAN BE.

The Loving Little Rituals of Romance

Is it really a mystery why half of all marriages end in divorce? To some people, it's an even bigger mystery how couples who *are* happy in their marriages get—and more important, stay—that way.

It's not a mystery to us. It's actually rather simple: if you want a long-lasting, happy marriage, you have to *do* something about it. But what exactly should you do? That's what this book is about. Based on more than fifteen years of research on marriage and family dynamics, we share the stories, habits, and activities of everyday happy couples. We tell you what we've learned about the things happy couples *do*. What they do every month, every week, and sometimes multiple times every day to connect with each other. More than anything, the stories will inspire you to do something to make your marriage happier. Better. More joyful.

So what *do* happy couples DO? They do things together. Do them repeatedly. Do them often. Happy couples develop and share couple rituals, connection rituals, or what we like to call the loving little rituals of romance. Rituals are the heartbeat of your marriage: steady, repeated, often taken for granted. They are the activities and interactions that, whether you're consciously aware of them or not, have symbolic importance in your relationship—the often mundane, daily activities that, if gone, would be missed; that say something about your unique history, outlook, or interests as a couple; that remind you of something you share as a couple; that reflect your "coupleness."

Many people ask if it's important to marry someone who shares the same religious upbringing or is the same age or has similar values and beliefs. The answer is no, no, and no. Researchers have identified no single model of the happily married couple. Happy couples come in all shapes and sizes, and from all religious backgrounds, ethnicities, and ages. They also take a variety of approaches to interacting with each other.

Research clearly shows that rituals strengthen and improve relationships. But this book is not so much about theorizing as it is about sharing the practical lessons learned from real-life couples living real-life marriages. We asked couples from all over the country, of all ages, and at all stages of life what made their marriages steady, strong, and happy. The stories they shared inspired us, touched us, and made us laugh, cry, and cringe (sometimes all at once). They are stories we simply can't keep to ourselves.

We wrote this book to share, inspire, and encourage. To share the beautiful and creative ways couples interact. To inspire you to develop your own little rituals, which can benefit your marriage in profound and long-lasting ways. To encourage you to embrace and protect the ways you already find ritual strength in your relationship. For rituals of connection will powerfully bond you, helping you create a marriage that will withstand the inevitable ups and downs of life.

This book will also teach you that you can DO something about the state of your marriage. Because if we've learned anything in our discussions with happy couples, it's that your marriage is truly up to you. All relationships require effort and intention. As marriage researcher William Doherty reminds us, "The key to growing a marriage ... is to be intentional about the connection rituals of everyday life."

Finally, this book will help you decide *what* to do—by showing you rituals that keep other couples happy, revealing rituals too private or embarrassing for couples to share themselves, and giving you ideas about how you and your spouse can remain happily connected (and married) for life. As you will see, most connection rituals don't require much effort or money, and all can be easily adapted, adopted, or taken for a test drive in your own marriage right now. The simplicity of it all will surprise and delight you. Enjoy.

PLAY TOGETHER OFTEN.
DO LAUGH.
CREATE FUN.

1 Belly Button Fuzz

It started one day when Samantha noticed some blanket fuzz in Mike's belly button and teased him about it. Soon she began routinely checking her husband's belly button for fuzz. If none appeared for a few days, Mike actually put some in his belly button for her to find.

More than ten years later, Samantha and Mike are still enjoying a daily search-and-rescue mission for belly button fuzz. And although unsavory to the outsider, Samantha has kept the multicolored collection of mini-fuzz balls in a small tin, a reminder of this playful ritual they share.

Why would anyone want to check another person's belly button for fuzz? Even better (or worse), keep those remnants in a tin? A bit disgusting? Maybe. Guaranteed to bring lifelong marital happiness? Not necessarily. But for one couple, it's a playful ritual that has bonded them over the years, giving them a fun connection at the end of each day.

Research shows that playfulness is a simple—and completely free!—way to increase your odds of having a happier, stronger marriage. Develop simple ways to enjoy your spouse at the end—or start—of each day. Play often. Because if you play together, you *are* more likely to stay together.

2 Twelve. Two. Ten.

We love going to the big movie theaters where there are twelve movies playing at once. We'll buy two tickets for something, for just anything, whatever time we show up at the place. We'll then go in and sit down, and sometime in the first ten minutes, if we don't like it, we get up and leave and try another movie. We just float around and sometimes try out ten different movies until we find something we like! It's a great adventure.

Don't forget that in marriage *you* get to choose. Not just the movie, but also the script. The script of your marriage. The lines, the plot, the story of what you want your relationship to be. (Is it a romantic adventure or a horror film?) Whether you want it to last twelve minutes, two months, or ten years (or sixty!), DO recognize that you play a significant role in determining if your marriage is a blockbuster (or simply a bust).

3 No One Else Exists

On most Sunday evenings in the summer we get a babysitter, pack a picnic (a crisp bottle of white wine is a must), head downtown, find a spot on the grass, and enjoy an outdoor concert by the local symphony orchestra. Although we're surrounded by hundreds of other kids, families, and couples, it's like we're on a first date again, enjoying each other as if no one else exists.

What's the underlying signature of your marriage? Although it's a complex phenomenon built on weeks, years, or decades of shared history, your marriage has a core. A signature. Did you know that your connection rituals—the Sunday evening picnic, the Saturday morning cup of coffee, the Monday evening stroll around the neighborhood—are significant in revealing that signature? What you're about? What your marriage truly *is*? Your repeated activities are not just a sign of what you enjoy as couple, they reveal and create your very essence as a couple.

DO recognize your rituals. Make an effort to sustain them. If that means hiring a babysitter or taking turns watching the kids with your friends or neighbors, do it! Rituals provide equilibrium and imply a future. Regardless of their form, they all serve a similar function. Make sure you protect and enjoy as many as you can so that you can function as a couple as well as you can … as if no one else exists … as if no one else matters (at least for one concert, at least for one date, at least for one moment).

4 A Volley of Kisses

*" My husband and I blow kisses to each other in the dark
at bedtime. We used to think it was a sort of loving laziness.
(We didn't want to roll over after we were all cozy in our positions
and ready to sleep.) But it's become something rather fun and
playful. We kiss, pause, and then blow. Then the other makes a
kissing sound and blows. We sometimes do this back and forth,
like a volley of kisses, for a few minutes before finally saying 'Good
night, Sweetie. Good night.'"*

Over time, it is (unfortunately) quite natural to become lazy in
our love. In our lives. In our relationships. This couple reveals how they
have transformed laziness into loving playfulness. What simple lesson
can you learn from them about your own life? Your own love? Your loving
relationship? Take note of areas of laziness. Make them opportunities
for loving-ness.

Fuzzy Rug

When Lorraine comes home from her monthly card night with friends, she always finds a practical joke waiting for her. One time her husband, Ed, bundled up several pairs of socks and tucked them under the covers on her side of the bed. Exhausted, Lorraine stumbled into bed only to find that something else was occupying her spot. She yelped as Ed kept still, holding back laughter. The following month, Ed hid a fuzzy rug underneath the covers. Again, Lorraine shrieked as Ed lay quietly snickering at her little surprise in the middle of the night.

Ed always keeps Lorraine guessing—and laughing. The couple met years earlier when Ed sat behind Lorraine at the movies and provided comical running commentary about the scenes and characters. Lorraine recalls, "My friends and I were laughing so hard at this stranger behind us. We couldn't wait to see who it was!"

After nearly five decades of marriage, Ed is still making Lorraine laugh. He still finds ways to trick, surprise, and delight her.

What makes your partner laugh? How did you used to delight and surprise each other? Bring those moments back into your marriage.

Surprise Your Spouse. Make Marriage delightfully SUSPENSEFUL.

6 Kiss Kiss

Every once in a while, if I have a piece of paper that I'm going to throw away and I've just applied lipstick, I'll kiss it and put a little note on it, like 'Miss you' or 'Think of me.' Then I'll leave it in different places, like in his company truck or some other place he will find it. And he keeps them. He always keeps them. I'll find them later. Years later. A whole stack of them. Those little gestures obviously meant a lot.

Janice has developed this sweet, simple ritual that her husband, Joe, enjoys again and again at the most unexpected times and in the most unexpected places.

What might you do that is fun and surprising to your spouse? **DO** it today. Do it again tomorrow. If it's truly a treat, do it often. Because even though small acts of affection might seem insignificant, the accumulation can result in something significant indeed.

7 Top Model

Maura and Christopher watch their favorite TV shows together every night, but it's *America's Next Top Model* that gets them up and moving. After watching the models on the show attempt different looks and moves, Maura and Christopher stage their own competition, using their bedroom hallway as a runway. One by one they strut their stuff and pivot swiftly on the wood floor, taking cues from the models on the show. As they judge each other on their performances, they laugh deeply and heartily together.

What brings you and your spouse deep joy? What brings on the hearty laughter? If you don't know, find out. If you do, bring it on! Soon you and your spouse will be the *model* couple others will try to emulate.

BE BOTH NOVEL AND PREDICTABLE.

Embrace THE EXPECTED. ACCEPT THE UNEXPECTED.

Message in the Jar

"*Before our kids were old enough to read, we would try to be the first one to write (using a toothpick) a sexy little note in the undisturbed smooth finish of a new jar of peanut butter. It was always such a fun surprise to find 'I love your lips' or 'Meet me upstairs at 8:30' when you unscrewed the peanut butter lid for the first time. We usually bought the smallest peanut butter jars so we had the opportunity to write more notes. Now that our kids can read, we still do this, but the notes are much less 'interesting.'*"

Try to become aware of how your daily routines—both the mundane and the extraordinary—give you and your spouse the chance to experiment yet feel comforted, to know what's expected while exploring the unexpected, to be both novel and predictable.

DO find a way to carve a little love (or love note) into your day. Into your spouse's day. Into the jar of night cream, creamy peanut butter, or can of shortening (if you must). You never know what kind of message you might get in return.

Sing Me the Day

Every night before we go to sleep, Maria makes up a song about the things that happened during the day. The song even rhymes! She sings a song like this almost every night. And I listen.

Carlos and Maria has evolved a playful and harmonious way to end the day, requiring just three ingredients: a little bit of rhythm, a lot of creativity, and one willing audience member.

Although you may not be able to compose a song for your spouse, ask yourself these poignant questions:

Where's the rhythm in your relationship?

What do you want the tempo to be?

Recognize that you can do a lot to set or change the tone.

The Kissing Rule

"Whenever we're on a long trip together and it's time to switch drivers, we pull over, get out, and run around the car doing a 'fire drill.' What makes this special is our rule that we have to kiss each time we run into each other. It's especially fun to steal a smooch in winter when we're running around outside of our warm car without our coats on!"

DO something to switch your regular routines into more joy-filled rituals. DO something that will shift a mindless event into a mind-exhilarating one (or at least one that you don't mind as much).

Most of us are busy. We spend a lot of time running in different directions from our spouse. Why not try purposefully running *into* your spouse? And when you do, declare it a rule that whenever you are in this spot, you get to steal a smooch. Like the couple above, initiate a rule that kissing is a must. Somewhere. Sometime. This is one rule you'll likely be more than happy to follow. Can't hurt to try, can it?

11 Naked Dinner

Before we had our kids, we would occasionally have naked dinners. Now that the kids are around, we've had to find other ways to keep this kind of wild and crazy intimacy alive. And we've been doing OK, although we miss those days of being naked at (and then sometimes on) the dinner table.

This ritual needs no explanation. No lesson. No research to support its worth. If you and your spouse can bring yourselves to the table without your clothes on, you must be doing something right.

Honey, what's for dinner?

GIVE *FREELY*
TO EACH OTHER.
MODEL GENEROSITY.
PUT YOUR
SPOUSE FIRST
IN YOUR THOUGHTS
AND HEART.

A Flower a Day

"*Almost every day of our fifty-five years of married life, John comes in after wandering around the yard and says, 'I brought you the flower of the day!' Sometimes I'll catch a glimpse of him in the yard with an umbrella over his head walking in the rain or snow, eyes toward the ground. In winter he may bring me a pretty branch. In summer it might be a single flower. During the peak of spring bloom, a bunch of tulips. No matter what it is, I always make a point to give him a kiss and a hug to acknowledge him and the flower. And I always put it in a nice vase rather than just a jar. It's the little things that matter to us.*"

Gestures in long-lasting marriages need not be extravagant. Something simple—every day—can keep a marriage healthy. What do you and your partner do—the small gestures—that pay homage to your history and partnership? What *could* you do?

13 Your Call

Many happy couples make an effort to simply call or e-mail each other at least once during the day. Sometimes it's just a quick hello. Sometimes it's a more lengthy conversation. But a call can say "I care" or "I want to be in touch" or "I like that you're in my life." One couple we know looks forward to a quick call at 8:30 each morning. Jeff calls home at about that time every morning just to check in, his wife, Kathy, explains. It's not so much the content of the call that matters but the fact that he calls.

Why not find a sacred time to call or e-mail your spouse each day? The *message* it sends is likely much more important than what you actually *say*.

IT'S THE LITTLE THINGS.

14 Underwear Duty

My husband thinks it's his job to make sure my underwear is even on both sides of my rear end. At first this was irritating. But when it stopped, I missed it. It was a little thing that kept us connected, even though it's kind of silly. And we both know he doesn't care all that much about the underwear, but he loves having a reason to touch my rear end.

Terry takes his duty seriously. If Lori's underwear is off even a bit, he adjusts it. Writer Sandy Broyard notes, "In the marriage that endures, there is no need for grandiosity." Find pleasure in even the smallest gestures, jobs, and routines of your marriage. There you will find your greatest joys.

In the marriage that endures there is no need for *grandiosity*.

— Sandra Broyard

15   Gretchen's Gas

Gretchen's husband, Sam, always fills up her car with gas. He does so, he says, because she simply doesn't like the smell of gas on her hands.

Similarly, Carlos does a number a little things for his wife, Megan, that make a big difference:

He spoils me dreadfully. I'll be in the bathroom, and he'll knock on the door and ask, 'Can I bring you a cup of coffee? Want a piece of toast?' Or he'll sneak in the bedroom and make the bed quick before I can get it done.

In marriage we sometimes stew about why our partner isn't kinder, nicer, more thoughtful. Instead of stewing, begin DOing. Imagine what your relationship could be like if you shifted your attitude (and actions) and began doing things *for one another*, instead of just getting them done.

Happy couples emphasize the way little efforts make huge differences in their marriages. Life is busy. Think about what can make your spouse's life a little less so. In doing so, you'll make your marriage more of what you want it to be and less of what you don't.

Always Always

One thing we NEVER do is go to bed alone. Ever. I don't go upstairs and get in bed and then Robert comes up later. Or vice versa. When we go to bed, we both go to bed. Together. We always, always go to bed together.

This couple's bedtime sync is quite remarkable. Not because they can both enjoy the restorative powers of sleep at the same time. But because they have recognized how the simplest of gestures, the simplest coordination, can create something quite magical in their marriage.

Try it. You might be surprised and delighted at how comforting it can be to always (always) do certain activities, make certain choices, or approach certain parts of your day with the soothing predictability of knowing you'll never (never) be doing it alone. That you can always (always) know what to expect. That you're making a gesture that says you are always (always) putting your spouse first in your thoughts and heart.

DO RECOGNIZE
THE COMFORT
OF THE WHOLE THING.
THIS THING CALLED
MARRIAGE.

17 Clip. Clip.

My husband always cuts my toenails. I don't know when it started, but he's always cut my toenails for me. It's not that I can't do it, but he just always has. It might sound gross, but it's very sweet.

Together you and your spouse have created something greater than the sum of your parts. It's not a fifty-fifty deal—it's a big deal that requires you both to extend a lot of effort a lot of the time. And the efforts don't need to be grand (or gross, for that matter). The smallest efforts can result in the biggest returns. Whether it's a little clip of the toenail here or a little fix of the underwear there. Whether it's filling up the gas tank here or putting a little toothpaste on the toothbrush there.

Marriage is what you make it, so DO make it great by clipping, gassing, fixing, pasting … whatever your marriage needs … or whatever does it for *your* spouse, *your* relationship. And if you haven't figured out what *it* is, make that your first priority.

MARRIAGE

IS IN THE DOING.

EVERY DAY.

18 There's Woody

"When we were first married and lived in a different part of the country, we rented a little house while we were finishing graduate school. In our backyard was a woodpecker that tapped the most delightful sounds for us throughout the day. Sometimes it was the first sound of the morning. Sometimes it was during dinner. Sometimes it was late in the evening. Every spring when the weather warmed, 'Woody' returned. And every spring we'd each try to be the first to hear his tapping and say, 'There's Woody!' A few years after we'd moved to another part of the country, one of the first things we heard was the sound of a woodpecker tapping away at a tree right outside our house. 'There's Woody!' Although we knew it wasn't 'our' Woody, the sound of a woodpecker to this day makes us pause, smile, and remember our first home and our first years of marriage."

As marriage researcher William Doherty observes, "Almost anything can be turned into a ritual of connection if the focus is on the relationship." What is the "Woody" in your life that you may be taking for granted? What have you been overlooking, missing, or simply too content (or bored) to notice? Are you guilty of failing to pause? Failing to take notice?

DO focus on your relationship by turning even the most obvious or mundane aspects of your daily life (the woodpecker outside your window, the undisturbed new jar of peanut butter, the toenails that need clipping) into a most magnificent ritual of connection.

THE simplest

OF GESTURES

ARE OFTEN

THE MOST MAGICAL

IN MARRIAGE.

Invisible Bond

My parents, married over fifty years now, have celebrated most of them in wedded bliss. But it hasn't come easy. They've worked hard taking care of each other. In the early years of their marriage, my mom would slip notes into my dad's briefcase or hide a little hello in his suit pocket for him to discover during the day. And naturally, during those years, Mom did all the cooking, cleaning, and ironing—what was traditionally expected in 'taking care of your man' during their generation. Today it's Dad's turn. He takes loving care of his eighty-year-old bride, who faces a number of health problems. Even though he's eighty-six, he rises early every morning, prepares the coffee, then gently awakens 'his love' with a freshly brewed cup and a donut hole, alongside the many medications she needs first thing in the morning. His loving attention continues throughout the day—every day—as he cares for my mom in the selfless way that only the love of a life would (and could) do.

To set the tone in your marriage, consider what author Robert Fulghum observes: that conversation and interaction between people create a covenant, an invisible bond. Just two people working out what they want, what they believe, what they hope for each other.

The work of marriage happens in the everyday moments. The how-was-your-day conversation. The cup of coffee. The medicine. The donut hole. The most mundane occurrences of our lives.

DO make sure you're not missing those moments by thinking only about what could be. Should be. Ought to be. Once was. Recognize that this *is* it. These moments *are* your marriage. That doesn't mean you can't do them better, differently, more thoughtfully. What it does mean is that your invisible bond is being tightened or undone through and by these conversations. These events. These gestures. Little by little. Forever and ever.

Nurture your Invisible Bond.

Little by Little.

Forever and Ever.

Bare-Chested Hugs

Joe and Natalie have crafted—and even given a name to—a brief but intimate connection ritual they share each morning:

My husband insists on having a hug before I put my clothes on in the morning. They're called bare-chested hugs.

Another couple has found a similar way to be close each morning:

After my husband showers and shaves early in the morning, he comes back into bed for hugs and kisses before dressing. What a great way to start each day before each of us goes to work. It originated on our honeymoon.

Intimacy is the cornerstone of healthy relationships. Research consistently shows that being physically intimate with your partner—even in nonsexual ways—is crucial for fostering the emotional connection that helps sustains marriages in the long run.

Unfortunately, many couples believe that intimate moments should be reserved only for certain times or certain spaces. But intimate gestures need not be grandiose. Although your intimacy rituals will wax and wane over time, find ways to create and nurture even brief moments and small gestures of intimacy in your daily interactions. Find what works. Make it happen.

21 Back Scratch to Basics

For the past twenty years or so, Kamar has been scratching Adara's back as she falls asleep at night:

It's the best thing to go to sleep and relax with someone scratching my back. Each night around nine o'clock, I climb into bed and turn to Kamar. 'OK, now it's your time to scratch my back.'

And so he does. He scratches. Even after Kamar battled a rare disease that injured his "back-scratching" arm, he continued to do what she loved—a simple light scratching of her skin—every night. Because it was one of the basics of their marriage and a daily ritual they both counted on, the first night he was home from the hospital Kamar stood at Adara's bedside to scratch with his healthy arm.

What are the basics in your marriage? Think about what would happen if they were gone. Then make sure to appreciate and protect them before they are.

GET BACK
TO THE **BASICS**
OF YOUR
RELATIONSHIP.

Tightly Wound Rope

" While we are lying on the couch together watching TV or reading, Ben always twirls my hair around his pointer finger. He does it until the hair is as tight as can be, like a thick section of rope. I love the feeling of it ... a calming way to unwind at the end of the day. Then I have to watch out because he will stick the tip of my hair—the pointy end of the tightly wound rope—up my nose! It makes us laugh every time, especially when he really gets it in there. "

Any physical connection can become a cherished ritual in your day. Like the husband who lovingly twirls his wife's hair, small gestures can create treasured moments.

DO make sure you physically connect with your spouse every day. If you're not sticking hair up his or her nose, then pluck out some belly button fuzz or simply rub each other's aching feet. Where else in life can you just be yourself, with the comfort of knowing you don't have to impress and you won't be judged? Create that place in your marriage.

CREATE FREQUENT WAYS OF *connecting* WITH EACH OTHER.

23 Bridge Your Lips

Whenever we're out on a walk or hiking, we always kiss on the bridges. If we're on our bicycles, we stop and get off. This originated on our first date—our first kiss was on a bridge—and we've been doing it ever since.

This couple created their kissing ritual to remind them of their first date more than thirty years earlier. It also helps them create a strong future.

Why not develop a ritual that will recreate (again and again) your first kiss? Or why not just develop a ritual that will encourage you and your spouse to kiss anytime (again and again)?

Hands in the Darkness

" Every night we go to bed, find each other's hands in the darkness, and pray out loud together, asking God to guide and protect our family, grant us restful sleep, watch over our friends in need, and help with any other needs that arise. This is the most important ritual of our day, together in prayer. "

Although you may not pray out loud in your marriage, you can surely find a way to reach for your spouse's hand, whether it's in the darkness of night or during the middle of the day, at a very public event or during a private moment on the sofa. Try it. You might find that even the lightest touch will warm your souls and rekindle a powerful sense of what you marriage once was … and surely can be again.

TALK.
CHAT.
CONVERSE.
DEVELOP
A PRIVATE CODE.

(· · · ___ ___ ___ ___ · · ·)

25

The Tempered Toothbrush

"*Whoever goes in the bathroom and brushes their teeth first always puts toothpaste on the other's toothbrush. When you get in there and the toothpaste is not there, you're like, 'Are you mad at me or what?' That's always the first question.*"

Can a toothbrush keep your marriage (as well as your gums) healthy? For this couple, toothbrush and paste placement opens the door to more difficult questions, such as "What's wrong?" or "Can we talk?"

Another couple developed an almost identical system:

"*I'll put Margaret's toothpaste on her toothbrush, or she'll put it on mine if she's the first one in the bathroom. It's a little sign that we don't have any problems with one another that day. If we're upset with one another, we might set the tube next to the brush and not put paste on it.*"

For both of these couples, the toothbrush serves as a private sign. It's also often an invitation to enter an important conversation.

Do you have the equivalent of a toothbrush in your relationship? If so, does it help initiate productive and healthy conversations about how you're feeling about the other person or what's upsetting you? Sometimes a "code" can be a nonthreatening way to ensure that you check in with your spouse every day. If you don't have one already, think of a private way to ask your spouse, "How ya doin' today?"

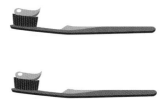

Private Language

" My husband calls himself my secret lover. When he sends me a card, he always signs it 'Your Secret Lover.' And he jokes that he's sure I don't know who it is! "

Another couple uses the phrase "I.U." as shorthand for "I love you."

Yet another man reveals, "My wife calls me 'Pup' because we live in an apartment and can't have a dog. Or she'll call me 'Lucky Pup.' So when I give her a card, I always sign it 'Pup' and leave a little paw print."

Marriage researchers have studied extensively the way couples nurture a sense of "we-ness" through the use of private language. By sharing a personalized set of words or gestures, couples not only communicate more efficiently, but they also create a "culture of two." Called idiosyncratic communication, private language includes nicknames as well as more elaborate ways of communicating that only the two of you understand (like the toothpaste set next to the brush).

What private nicknames, language, or gestures have you and your partner devised? How do they give you a unique way to connect?

CREATE A CULTURE
OF TWO.

Pillow Fight

We keep our pillows in the linen closet. If I'm not really pleased with Barry, I don't get his pillow out when we go to bed. And he'll say, 'Where's my pillow?' But he knows what it means. It's our way of letting each other know how we're feeling about each other. It's a way to get some stuff out on the table that we need to talk about.

Most marriage researchers agree that constructive communication is the single best predictor of happy marriages. The ability to productively express anger or even mild irritation is one of the most important skills a couple can develop. For Barry and Anita, a "pillow fight" provides a healthy way to initiate conversation about feelings or observations that are hard to bring up otherwise.

Do you and your spouse express your irritation and anger productively? If not, find a way to DO so. And then do so gently. Do so with understanding. If you can, do so with little defensiveness and lots of willingness.

Cuddle Bumps & Corn Chip

The following is a list of actual nicknames couples use for each other:

Attic Breath	Hoki Fish	Pooh Bear
Baby Doll	Jillybean	Pookey Pie
Big Daddy Rabbit	Jimbo	Post-'em
Boobala	Lassie	Puddin'
Bootie	Little Sausage	Queen Diamond
Bun	Littles	Rapster
Bunnie Mae	Loopy	Ritzy
Buttercup	Louigee	Rotunda
Care Bear	Love-Cheese	Rufflepuffle
Cherry	Moo	Sneezy
Chubby	Nancy Drew	Snugglebutt
Colonel Sanders	Nit	Sparky
Corn Chip	Nude	Spook
Cuddle Bumps	Parcheesi	Stinker
Curtle	Patty Pooh	Sugar Lump
Fez	Peeper	Sushi
Girdle	Pez Jug	Sunshine
Hunka-Munka	Poochy	Zaddy

What's in a name? A lot, according to researchers. Especially nicknames. Using nicknames with your spouse not only reveals your creativity but can actually strengthen your marriage. How? Nicknames are shorthand for saying, "I know you in a way no one else does." They create that sense of privacy and "we-ness." If you don't already have a special name for your spouse, craft one. Or feel free to steal one or two from the list on the preceding page. We don't mind. And who will know anyway … they're private!

DO CREATE

MAGIC

FROM YOUR

ME + YOU.

29

Me + You = "Mu"

Newlyweds Anne and Brendan were having one of their not-so-unusual-but-very-much-appreciated discussions about the future: "When we will have children?" "Will we buy a house soon?" "What are our dreams?" During a loving and emotional moment in that conversation, Brendan whispered, "I love me and you." Anne, in a tongue-twisted moment, replied, "I love mu, too."

To this day, the phrase serves as their private salutation, farewell, and idiosyncratic expression of affection. On the way out the door: "I love mu!" Hanging up after a brief conversation: "I love mu." In a moment of comfort or joy: "I love mu so much."

DO recognize how much more interesting and robust the equation of marriage is when you add Me to You. Do you recognize the product of what you've created together? If it's not adding up currently—and it won't from time to time—make an effort to get it back to the "Mu" you started with.

Hot Dog!

We look for dogs wherever we go, and I always compare them to my dog, Star. But the other dogs never measure up! And if we see a dog on TV or anywhere else, it usually reminds me of something that happened with Star and me, and then I'll have to retell that story. I call these stories 'Star stories.' Brian's job is just to sit there and make fun of the story or laugh like it really happened. Because these stories have titles like 'Star Saved the World!'

Brian and Sauri turned their love of dogs into a shared symbol and playful game in their relationship. They don't currently own a dog, but they enjoy laughing about dogs they see, talking about others' dogs, and reminiscing about Sauri's former dog.

Couples who share symbols tend to be stronger, happier couples, say relationship researchers.

What holds special meaning to just the two of you? A song? A rock from your first date? A tin of fuzz plucked from your spouse's belly button?

Make an effort to embrace the items, objects, or interests that symbolize your history, your present, and your shared sense of the world. They don't just make your relationship strong—they actually help make your relationship what it is.

Will You Please Squeeze My...

This is something my husband and I have been doing since we were dating (more than fifteen years ago). He used to have oily skin and get these great zits on his back. I'd beg him to let me go after them. Eventually he did. Then it became a regular routine! As for me, I get the occasional butt zit that I make him get. He pretends it grosses him out, but he always goes after it with great enthusiasm.

If there's anything more gross than picking each other's belly button fuzz, it's got to be picking each other's zits. But marriage researchers would say this couple is doing something very right. Betsy and Greg understand and appreciate their vocabulary of affection.

Happy couples figure out the "relational currencies" in their marriage. They develop a common vocabulary, verbal or nonverbal, of caring. They learn how the other person wants to be loved. They discover the activities and behaviors each perceives as affectionate.

Happy couples come to an agreement—often over years of trying and failing, and usually without ever being explicit—about their language of love.

To some, vacuuming equals love. ("When he vacuums without being asked, it really means a lot."). To others, listening equals love. ("When she really tunes in and listens to my ranting at the end of the day, I can tell how much she cares.") To yet others, food equals love. ("When I come home to find my favorite meal of pork tenderloin and asparagus just coming off the grill, I know how much I'm loved.") And yes, to some (maybe more than would admit it), zit popping equals love.

What is your language of love? If you don't know, DO find out. And soon.

Every Friday we have a discussion where we acknowledge successes and little extras we've done throughout the week. Sometimes it's just a 'thank you' to the other person. Sometimes it's noticing a good effort or a small victory. For example, last week I acknowledged my husband for doing extra morning dishes and for being honest and up-front with his boss. Before it's his turn to acknowledge my successes, I ask him what I might have missed: what does he want to be acknowledged for? Then we switch.

How well a couple communicates largely determines how satisfying or unsatisfying a marriage is. But not all communication is created equal. Knowing what kind of communication to pay attention to—and what to minimize—is the trick. Researchers like John Gottman have spent decades trying to determine exactly which types of communication put your marriage on a trajectory toward divorce and which kind don't matter as much. For example, complaining isn't in and of itself bad for a marriage.

This couple avoids two of the most corrosive communication behaviors in marriage—criticism and defensiveness—by creating a venue for two very healthy behaviors—positivity and openness. By avoiding criticism and defensiveness, they are also much less likely to spiral into three other destructive communication patterns that have been shown to predict divorce: contempt, withdrawal, and hostility.

DO try to outlaw the five most corrosive kinds of communication in your marriage:

Criticism

Contempt

Defensiveness

Withdrawal

Hostility

If these do rear their ugly heads, note that they are present and quickly find alternative ways of expressing yourselves. When you can minimize or avoid such behaviors altogether, the victory will be anything but small.

NOT ALL
COMMUNICATION IS
CREATED EQUAL.
KNOW WHICH
KIND DESERVES
ATTENTION IN
YOUR MARRIAGE.

Elephant Shoes

Do you and your spouse have a private way of saying "I love you?" If not, you might want to invent one. We found that most happy couples express their love verbally, often in an idiosyncratic or unique way. Like the couple who uses the phrase "elephant shoes" for "I love you." Other phrases, gestures, and words couples told us they use to say "I love you" include:

A wink
A double wink
Three hand squeezes
A quick hand squeeze
Touching fingertips
Curling the pointer finger
A "cluck cluck" sound
A scratch above the ear
"Bunches"

"Me too."
"4"
"Noodle"
"Loon you"
"I.U."
"Sagapo"
"Te quiere"
"Only You"
"Me More"

Or how about three hand squeezes ("I love you") followed by two squeezes back ("How much?") followed by a big squeeze ("This much!")

Share Love.

Share Laughter.

Share a Little

and a Lot.

A Little Dash Will Do It

"*Whenever we go shopping (for anything—groceries, shoes, a movie rental), we get out of the car, pause to look at each other, then race each other to the store. We sprint to the door, running as fast as we can to be the first one to touch the entrance of wherever we are shopping. My husband always wins (he was a track star). But once we've made it, we laugh and laugh and feel like kids all over again. We don't really care that other people stare at us. We could be in the worst mood, but after a fifty-yard dash (or four-hundred-meter sprint) we're both smiling again.*"

DO get more actively engaged in your marriage by finding even one activity you both enjoy—bargain hunting, cooking, cleaning out the basement, playing cards, running like track stars—and commit to doing that activity again as if it's the first time you've ever done it. You'll soon see how beautiful this thing called marriage was meant to be—and can be again with a little bit of time, a little bit of effort, and (why not?) a little bit of healthy competition!

35 No Sense in Worrying

How my wife feels really affects how I feel. For instance, she worries too much. And even though I always tell her, 'No sense in worrying about that because it's not going to change it,' she worries anyway. And that's OK. Because if she's happy, I'm happy. And if she's not very happy, then I feel, you know, not happy. That's the comfort of being a couple ... sharing it all together.

The opposite of love isn't hate, it's apathy. And the opposite of empathy is selfishness. In marriage, there is little room for selfishness, no room for apathy, and lots of room for knowing that you have a partner willing to experience what you experience and feel what you feel without expectation or judgment.

DO notice how your spouse's feelings affect yours. If that annoys you, try embracing it instead of denouncing it. Your long history together provides one of the most wonderful comforts of being a couple: having each other to *share* in the happiness, the worry, the joy, the sorrow.

36 Kitchen Things

I think the best time we have together—the most important part of the day for us—is when we come home from work and do kitchen things together. We cook, we do the dishes, we clean up. We're together. Nothing special. It's our time to unwind from the day. And sometimes we don't even communicate. It's just being together, side by side.

DO value just being together. Two in one space. Recognize and embrace the comfort of the *whole thing*: this thing called marriage.

DO VALUE BEING.
TOGETHER.
TWO TOGETHER.
IN ONE SPACE.

Plain Old Wit

" My husband and I have been married thirty-six years and work together in our mom-and-pop business. Side by side, all day long. And we ride to and from work together. Every day. Since that's more than plenty of quality time for any couple, we've developed a little unspoken rule to keep it from getting stale. It's his job to make me laugh. Whether it's on our early morning drive, in between clients, or after supper, he rises to the occasion and makes me chuckle, giggle, or explode with a deep belly laugh. He's always coming up with new words, antics, or creative observations. Often it's just plain old wit. "

Happy couples establish norms for a range of issues: Who drives? Who does the laundry? Who's in charge of dry humor and plain old wit?

DO make sure you're not letting your relationship—your side-by-sidedness—get stale. If your relationship norms are not working, change them. Make a rule, create a routine, develop a way—whatever you need to do to keep your relationship alive and interesting.

Daisies or Dandelions?

In the spring and summer, one of our favorite activities is planting flowers and building the flower beds together. We get so much satisfaction from working on our home and seeing the progress of our work. It definitely brings us closer. It wouldn't be nearly as satisfying if we were doing this work alone.

Marriage researcher Judy C. Pearson found that couples who were happiest with their marriage and stayed married the longest tended to have lower expectations for their marriage. We're not suggesting you lower your expectations about marriage in general (although that can be helpful at times). Rather, realize that your level of satisfaction is directly related to your level of expectation. If you expect daisies but get dandelions, you'll be disappointed. The reverse is also true: if a beautiful flower pops up where a weed once grew, you'll be delighted.

DO lower your expectations a little so that your happiness can be a little greater. And expect the weeds. For if you do, they won't be such a disappointment when they do pop up (because, without a doubt, they will).

DO MAKE

YOUR EXPECTATIONS

A LITTLE LOWER

SO THAT

YOUR HAPPINESS

CAN BE

A LITTLE GREATER.

39 Magazines on the Floor

"As we lie in bed together, my husband and I often think of things we need to do the next day: 'I have to bring that file for Bob!' 'Don't forget that we need to e-mail Gina about this weekend.' 'The garbage is being picked up early this week because of the holiday. Remind me to put it out in the morning, will you?' Instead of trying to remember what we talked about, one of us will grab a magazine—any old magazine—from the bedside table and toss it into the middle of the floor. When we wake up in the morning and see the magazine there, we immediately remember the conversation and the 'to-dos' we mentioned."

This couple's creative and practical magazine toss illustrates the way happy couples work: together. As a unit. Mutually. As one. Research reveals that in successful marriages, there is mutual accountability. Each spouse takes responsibility for how happy the marriage is and how well it works.

Although happy couples may seem to come by their happiness naturally, almost effortlessly, don't be fooled. It takes intention to develop systems for working together. Happy couples have met (and overcome) difficulties. Happy couples see obstacles as opportunities for clarifying their core values. When happy couples stumble, they continue on their way. Their mutual goals yield great rewards.

DO work *one-fully* with your spouse. Adopt the spirit of mutual accountability for all aspects of your day. Your relationship. Your life. And when you toss magazines on the floor, do it intentionally, together.

DO COMMIT
TO CONTINUE,
TO OVERCOME,
TO FACE,
EVEN EMBRACE
YOUR CHALLENGES
AS A COUPLE.

Doing the Sidestroke

After decades of enjoying conversation while walking, biking, and playing tennis together, Mike and Rosa had to change their exercise routine to better suit their aging knees and hips. To adapt, they began swimming together at the local pool. But they quickly discovered that this new activity did not lend itself to conversation. So they adapted again by doing the sidestroke instead of the front crawl, which allowed them to face each other and talk while swimming. As they swim, Mike and Rosa chat about their kids, their day, and sometimes just what's for dinner. When they get to the other end of the pool, they both flip the other way and turn toward each other again.

When life presents new challenges, happy couples adapt. They find a way to flip, turn, or adjust, however so slightly. What can you do to better meet the needs of your marriage? To flip around and face your partner? If you've been doing the front crawl in your marriage, try the sidestroke instead.

WHAT CAN YOU DO TO FLIP OR TURN TOWARD YOUR SPOUSE?

Giving. Getting.

During their empty-nest years, Ruth and Don began working on a service project in their community. They helped open a hospice house for people with terminal illnesses and their families:

It's really meaningful to do something like this at this time in our lives. Though we are busy, we have the time. We no longer have the demands of raising children. We've already done that, and done it well. But now is another time ... a time for giving back.

This couple is contributing not only to a healthier community but also to a healthier marriage. At a time when many couples face the challenge of tuning back into their relationship after years of primarily tuning into their children, Ruth and Don recognized a common passion for a community concern.

Find something you and your spouse are both passionate about in your town, city, or schools. Commit your joint energies. And then notice how working together brings you closer to the community *and* to each other.

Good and Stubborn

When our youngest son went off to college, we started going to work earlier and coming home later. We were throwing ourselves into our work because there wasn't this necessity to get home earlier like before. Then we had one of those 'a-ha' moments when we realized that just because you don't have kids at home doesn't mean you shouldn't come home. We have our marriage to take care of now.

One of the key characteristics of couples in happy and enduring marriages, research shows, is stubbornness. Yes, couples who are good and *stubborn* about keeping their marriages strong and healthy through the inevitable ups and downs report the happiest and most stable marriages.

Next time you're experiencing even the slightest threat to your marriage, do bring on the stubbornness. DO something about whatever is happening. Change jobs. Hire babysitters. Move. Get new friends. Come home earlier. No one else is going to do it for you, so you need to do it yourself. This is one time when being stubborn is essential.

BE STUBBORN

ABOUT MAKING YOUR

MARRIAGE STRONG.

HEALTHY. HAPPY.

THEN DO WHATEVER

IT TAKES TO KEEP IT

THAT WAY.

43 And So It Begins...

Whenever we're leaving on a trip, one of us always turns to the other and portentously says, 'And so it begins ...'

Another couple shares a similar ritual:

Whenever we're getting home from a long trip, we always utter the comforting and familiar phrase, 'Home again, home again, jiggity-jig.'

Coming and going. Leaving and returning. Straying and getting back on course. Marriage is a journey, one that requires direction, attention, and often some tricky navigation. Ideally, it is also a safe haven that provides each partner a sense of stability, like the comfort one feels returning home after being away for a long time.

According to relationship expert Steve Duck, you are at the helm of your relation-"ship." You make choices that, every moment, affect the course of your marriage. You express yourself in ways that influence the responses you get. Although the dynamics of a lifelong marriage are complex, you play a significant role in navigating the good, the bad, the mundane, and the extraordinary.

If you've veered off course, do something to help get you and your spouse back where you want to be, perhaps with the help of a licensed counselor or skilled therapist. Although the first twelve months (or even twelve years) might not be the best, the next twelve (or twenty or thirty) can be better. DO find a way to make your marriage exactly what you want it to be.

You are at the *helm* of your Relation*Ship*.

My husband tends to shut down when he's at his parents, especially as we sit at dinner and they ask endless, silly, often irritating questions. He just stops talking. He's done. He won't even talk to me! After many years of this, I finally described to him what it felt like to me—like walking up to a bank teller who suddenly pulls down a curtain and puts up a sign saying, 'Next Window Please.' I still have to talk, carry on the conversation, stay engaged, while he's behind the curtain.

Now we use the phrase 'Next Window Please' to help us through rough times. I'll say, 'Don't you next-window-please me!' Sometimes as I look across the room at him, he will pretend to pull down a curtain in front of his face, finishing with a little next-window finger gesture. It makes us laugh.

The truth is, it's much easier to have this issue out in the open and to have identified the pattern. We're much more able to find the humor in these situations now."

Next-window-pleasing your spouse is the equivalent of stonewalling or withdrawing, which is one of the most destructive patterns in marriage, especially if it happens in the heat of disagreement. Interestingly, eighty percent of next-window-pleasers are male, according to researcher John Gottman.

Take a lesson from the couple above, who successfully recognized a potentially harmful pattern in their relationship. Find a way, like them, to name the pattern and then develop a simple (and productive) way of dealing with the next-window-please times or tendencies in your marriage.

FEED YOUR MARRIAGE WITH POSITIVITY. WITH KIND WORDS. WITH LOVING KINDNESS.

45 Adam's Suit

It still makes Adam smile when I hang up his suit. When he comes home, he takes off his suit coat and trousers and lays them on a chair. I always come in later and neatly hang them up in his closet. He told me one day just how good it makes him feel that I do this little thing. He didn't ask me to do it. And I didn't say to myself: 'Oh, I love him, I'll put his clothes away.' I just do it because I enjoy it. And I enjoy knowing it makes him happy.

Research shows that positivity in marriage is contagious. Kind words. Loving gestures. A suit hung neatly in the closet. Each is likely to be responded to in kind. And guess what? Negativity is the same, but more insidious. Unkind words, critical observations, or an accusatory tone are likely to be reciprocated with more of the same. Our interactions create centrifugal forces—not unlike the pull you felt on the merry-go-round as a child.

Which force would you rather have prevail in your marriage? The safe, gentle pull of joy, kindness, and positivity? Or the wild spinning of negativity and contempt?

DO something today, every day, to choose the direction of your marital interactions. No matter how powerful the momentum of past days, years, or even decades, you get to make the choices for *this* day. Get off the merry-go-round of negativity. When you do, you will no doubt enjoy the ride once again.

46 | Banner Love

"We have an 'I love you' banner that we have given each other over and over in the weirdest ways. It's just this dumb plastic banner with multicolored lettering. One time I was having a really rotten day, and my husband, Sean, was gone. I reached in my coat, and there in the sleeve was the banner. We can go a month, two months, three months, and all of a sudden it appears again. We have put the banner in each other's pillowcases, glove compartments, and pants pockets. It's a way to surprise each other with a warm thought on good or bad days."

Although our spouses are the most important people in our lives, most of us spend our energy and time attending to other people (coworkers, children, friends) and demands (work, travel, house and yard). While it's natural and important to have spaces in your togetherness, it's also important to find ways to intentionally bridge those spaces. This couple did so with a two-dollar banner—a priceless way to say "I love you" when they are not together.

There are as many ways to say "I love you" as there are minutes in the day. Take a minute now to decide how you can make your partner feel loved during time apart.

TAKE A MOMENT

(OR MAKE A MOMENT)

TO ADORE

YOUR SPOUSE.

47 Wicky-Wacky Cake

" His favorite cake is 'wicky-wacky chocolate,' a rich, made-from-scratch cake—an old family recipe. So when I really, really, really, really like him, and he's really, really, really, really made me happy, I bake him a wicky-wacky cake. He knows I'm really happy with him when he gets a wicky-wacky cake. "

Why not honor the most prized person in your life by identifying that little something he or she really relishes ... really favors ... really savors. A little bit of energy toward "I really, *really* like you!" can go a long way in a marriage, since, as we all know, there are (quite naturally) many times we don't feel so much *like* toward the person we love the most.

DO something to make sure *like* and *love* are the words, thoughts, and feelings you both use, express, and experience really (really, really) often in your marriage.

Lick Like Hank

Elizabeth and Ryan's dog, Hank, sloppily displays his affection by licking a person's face, hands, or anything he can get his tongue on. One day Elizabeth leaned over and licked Ryan's cheek, trying out Hank's enthusiastic approach of expressing love.

Since then, licking has become their inside joke and, to many outsiders, a rather disgusting sign of endearment. Even at a party, if (they think) nobody is looking, Ryan and Elizabeth stick out their tongues and try to sneak a lick on the other's cheek. What if they're caught? They don't really care:

'Licking like Hank' is our way of saying 'I love you to pieces' or 'You make me happy.'

How do you let your spouse know that he or she makes you happy? Although licking isn't required, happy marriages DO require that you let each other know you are loved. Be sure your dog isn't doing a better job than you are at expressing affection.

Three Goods, Two Bads

" Each night we do the 'goods and bads.' We each tell a good thing from that day, such as, 'Today I finished a project at work that has made me crazy for the last couple of weeks.' Then we each share a bad thing ('Today while we were doing the dishes, you sounded kind of perturbed at me. What's up?'). We talk until we've each shared three goods and two bads. And we have rules: We cannot be angry, only happy that the other one is sharing. We must be one hundred percent honest. We must not go to sleep until we both have shared. And we must always end with a good! "

Marriage, life, relationships … aren't they all about dealing with goods and bads? According to marriage researcher John Gottman, happy couples tend to have five times as many positive moments as negative ones.

Happy marriages thrive on positivity; they wither with too much negativity. This couple has found a creative way to productively express both the good and the bad, which is all to the good.

Priceless Valentine

> "My parents don't have much money, and what they have they don't like to spend on things they think are frivolous. So on Valentine's Day they always go to a greeting card store together and pick each other out a card. They then read their cards out loud to each other. They also tell each other what they would have written in the card had they bought it. They get the sentiment without the expense and have developed a loving tradition that has been with them for many, many years."

Our long, treasured histories together. Aren't they priceless? It's easy to forget just how valuable they are when we're busy caring for our children, our homes, our cars, our careers. Take a moment to really honor your most valuable relationship: your relationship with your spouse.

You can invest in your marriage without spending a penny. Spend a little time and energy, right now, on your everyday valentine. Our marriages are simply what we make them, the product of what we invest in them, and the result of what we put into them. Ah, priceless indeed.

51 Stick 'Em Up

Because I'm so busy with school, work, and taking care of our home, my husband sometimes has to be a little assertive when trying to get me to slow down and connect with him. He's developed this funny little way of demanding a hug by saying 'Stick 'em up … this is a hug-up.' It's a great reminder for me to slow down and take time for him (and us). When he says this, I immediately throw my hands in the air and pause for a nice long hug.

Our interactions—day in, day out—create our relationships. They make our relationships either havens of love or zones of bitterness and dread. They can make us feel like we're in heaven or like we're being held prisoner.

What do you want your marriage to be? What do your daily interactions suggest it will become? It's not too late to change the tone today to make a difference in the overall tone—the climate—of your marriage. Is your marriage a prison? Or a joyful retreat? The answer truly is up to you.

WHAT YOUR MARRIAGE ONCE WAS IT CAN SURELY BE AGAIN.

Cold, Cold Mornings

I'm a long-distance runner and run year round, rain or shine, sleet or snow. On many winter days, I run in temperatures near zero or below. Before my wife goes to bed, if she knows the next morning is a running day for me, she puts my running gloves, hat, and socks on the radiator in our kitchen. When I wake up on cold, cold mornings and put on these toasty-warm clothes, it makes me smile.

"An ounce of prevention is worth a pound of cure." We all know the old adage. Did you apply it to your marriage? Preventive maintenance is essential in relationships; monitoring the rhythms of our interactions and weaving the basic fabric of intimacy are crucial. How do you interact to sustain the feeling that you and your partner share a common world? If not gloves on the radiator, what else do you do—or could you do—to raise the warmth, even if just a degree, in your marriage?

She's Always Right

"My mom, married to my dad for forty-five years, always makes two drinks at cocktail time (about an hour before dinner). Lots of ice in both glasses. Then Scotch for her and Jack Daniels for him. She places her glass in her right hand (because, she says, she's 'always right') and puts my dad's glass in her left. She walks into the family room and hands my dad his drink. He lifts his eyes from the crossword puzzle or newspaper, and they do their toast: lifting their glasses to each other and gently clinking them together as my mom leans over for a little kiss and they both say, 'Love you.' It's been the same for as long as I can remember. Every night. Forty-five years."

Take a moment to notice, to really observe, the person on your right. The person you go to sleep with every night. The person you wake up with every morning. The person who stood next to you at the altar and with whom you vowed to be until death do you part.

Can you appreciate the precious reality that it takes both a left and a right to make something balanced? To make it complete? And that in the strongest relationships, whether you are right (or left or top or bottom) doesn't really matter. In a loving partnership, the ability to cope with inevitable ups and downs … rights and wrongs … goods and bads … is the secret of being complete. Being balanced. Being forever.

CELEBRATE
EACH OTHER.
NOW.
ALWAYS.
AS OFTEN
AS YOU CAN.

54

Anniversary Contest

" We were married on the 26th of May. We have a monthly contest to see who can say 'Happy Anniversary' first on the 26th day of every month. The rules are: no waking your spouse; you can say it anytime after midnight; and it must be person to person (no written messages or answering machine messages). This game started the first month after we were married in 1968, and we have never missed a month. But we don't keep score! "

Although anniversary celebrations are wonderful annual rituals, Mark and Camille's monthly contest—one without winners or losers—allows them to more regularly (and playfully) salute their love.

The winner here is this couple; they have found a way to celebrate each other and their marriage more than just once a year. Can you think of a way you and your spouse might regularly celebrate your marriage?

55 Show Me Your Beans

When Jack is out in the garden, finishing his gardening or picking vegetables, he always shows me his beans. And his tomatoes. But he's most proud of the beans. He always shows them to me and I always rave. And I scrape out his beans for him so he can enjoy them. It's our little thing: the beans.

What are the beans in your marriage? What do you like to share and show off? Have you fallen into the trap of holding back information, events, or accomplishments that are important to you but that (you think) are not as significant to your spouse? Consider the result of such holding back over time.

DO share your triumphs, however minor, with your spouse. And then make sure to rave about, clap for, and share in the successes and accomplishments, however small, in his or her day. When you do—bean after bean—you will quickly discover (maybe rediscover) that your spouse is indeed your greatest fan. And you are indeed his or hers.

56 Begin Again

On our anniversary, or when we're just having a rough time or need to renew our perspective about our relationship, we return to the same restaurant where we had our first date. It takes us right back to where (and most important, why) it all started. Revisiting the history of our relationship gives us clarity not only about where we began, but also about things we are dealing with now.

How do you recall or relive the very beginning of your relationship? Although this couple celebrates the first moments of their relationship by returning to the actual place where their relationship began, you can "revisit" your beginnings without physically doing so.

Reflecting on the past can give clarity to the present and future. Think about what brought you and your partner together. What could you do for your marriage by revisiting—physically, conversationally, emotionally—where and when you first met? Fell in love? Knew that this was for life?

TURN UP THE JOY IN YOUR MARRIAGE.

Turn It Up

> *'Our' song is 'Tupelo Honey' by Van Morrison. Every time we hear it, we turn it up and sing out loud together. And if we're apart and one of us hears the song, we call each other and put the phone up to the radio or leave a voice message with the song playing in the background.*

Even if you don't have an "our song," you and your spouse can easily add a bit more harmony to your relationship. Try singing each other's praises every chance you get (out loud, to your spouse). Sing together (who cares if you're no good). Sing in the shower (even better if you're in there together). Sing to each other as you're falling asleep (it works well for children—why not adults?).

DO find some way to bring the joy and energy back into your voice as a couple. Do something that will make your hearts sing, whether that's dancing in the dining room, juggling during the dinner hour, or getting out your wedding album and laughing at the hairstyles and bridesmaid dresses. When you turn up the laughter and joy in your marriage, you'll automatically turn down the disconnectedness.

Selected Books on Marriage and Rituals

Doherty, William J. *Take Back Your Marriage: Sticking Together in a World That Pulls Us Apart*. Guildford Press, 2001.

Fulghum, Robert. *From Beginning to End: The Rituals of Our Lives*. Villard Books, 1995.

Gottman, J.M. & Declaire, J. *The Relationship Cure: A Five-Step Guide to Strengthening Your Marriage, Family, and Friendships*. Three Rivers Press, 2002.

Gottman, J.M., Gottman, J.S., & Declaire, J. *Ten Lessons to Transform Your Marriage: America's Love Lab Experts Share Their Strategies for Strengthening Your Relationship*. Three Rivers Press, 2007.

Gottman, J. M & Silver, N. *The Seven Principles for Making Marriage Work*. Orion Press, 2004.

Pearson, J.C. *Lasting Love: What Keeps Couples Together*. William. C. Brown, 1992.